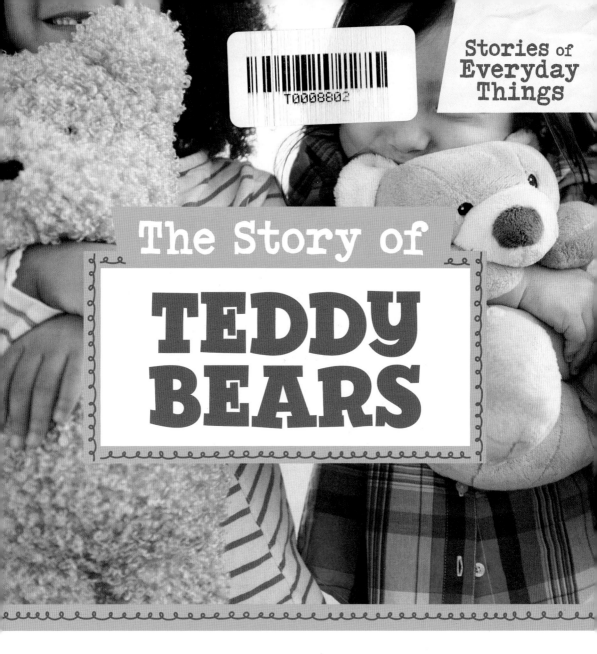

# The Story of TEDDY BEARS

by Mae Respicio

PEBBLE
a capstone imprint

Published by Pebble, an imprint of Capstone
1710 Roe Crest Drive, North Mankato, Minnesota 56003
capstonepub.com

Library of Congress Cataloging-in-Publication Data
is available on the Library of Congress website.
ISBN: 9780756577506 (hardcover)
ISBN: 9780756577872 (paperback)
ISBN: 9780756577568 (ebook PDF)

Summary: How are teddy bears made? What are they
made of? Who invented them? Find out everything you
ever wanted to know about teddy bears in this book.

Editorial Credits
Editor: Christianne Jones; Designer: Jaime Willems;
Media Researcher: Rebekah Hubstenberger; Production
Specialist: Whitney Schaefer

Image Credits
Alamy: Marijan Murat/dpa picture alliance, 17;
Dreamstime: David Calvert, 8; Getty Images: Christopher
Furlong, 11, iStock/halbergman, 23, iStock/ivanastar, 12,
iStock/Jelena83, 14, JGI/Jamie Grill, back cover, 1, khoa
vu, 5, Peter Dazeley, 26, Photos.com, 7, picture alliance,
15, Silke Woweries, 27, Thomas Niedermueller, 9, 18, 19,
21; Library of Congress: Prints and Photographs Division,
6; Shutterstock: Everett Collection, 10, Gorodenkoff, 24,
Helen89, 25, Julia Shauerman, 13, Lithiumphoto, 28,
Tee11, middle cover, The_Molostock, top cover, Variya, 20

Design Elements
Shutterstock: Pooretat moonsana, Luria

Printed and bound in China.    PO 5593

# Table of Contents

Words in **bold** appear in the glossary.

# History of Teddy Bears

People of all ages love teddy bears. They are cute. They are cuddly. They bring joy.

Teddy bears are so loved that almost half of the adults in America still have their teddy bears from childhood. But how did teddy bears begin?

The teddy bear began in an unlikely way. It began with a president! Theodore Roosevelt was the 26th president of the United States. His nickname was "Teddy."

In 1902, the president went on a hunting trip. He refused to shoot a bear. A newspaper published a cartoon about it.

DRAWING THE LINE IN MISSISSIPPI

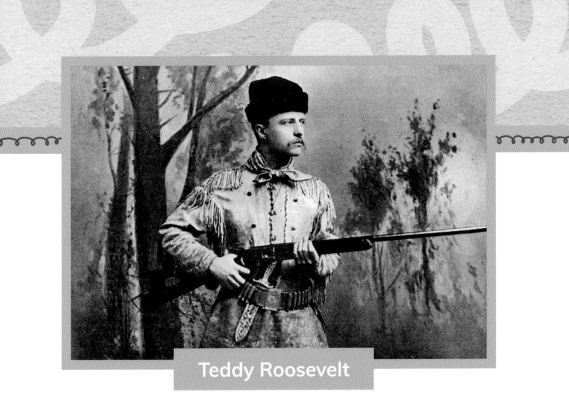

Teddy Roosevelt

To honor him, Morris and Rose Michtom made a stuffed bear. They asked if they could use his nickname. He agreed! They put the stuffed bear in a window with a sign that said *Teddy's Bear*. The Michtoms started a company to make toys and stuffed bears.

Around that time in Germany, Richard Steiff designed a stuffed bear. He made it out of **mohair**. His aunt, Margarete Steiff, owned a toy company. It sold felt toys. She added the stuffed bear to her store.

A teddy bear with the official Steiff label and button on its ear

At first, the product was not popular. But things changed after they shared it at a toy fair in Germany. An American ordered many to sell in the U.S. By 1907, a million had been made!

# Teddy Bears Then and Now

Early teddy bears were made by hand. Their eyes were made with buttons or glass. The problem? The parts were not safe. The eyes pulled off too easily.

A woman makes a teddy bear in the early 1900s.

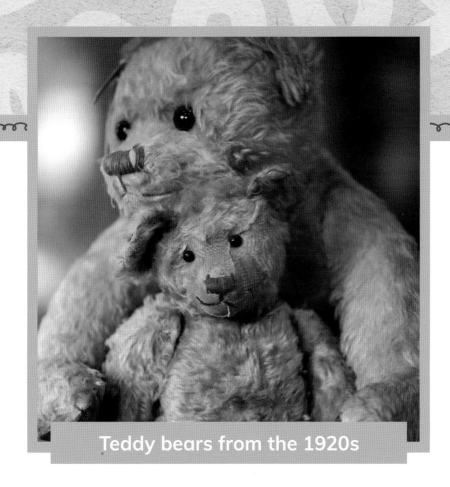

Teddy bears from the 1920s

Around 1950, teddy bears had safety features. The eyes could not pull off. Safety joints were used to help the arms and legs move. They looked similar to how we know them today.

# How Teddy Bears Are Made

Teddy bears can still be made by hand. But most are made in factories. Some of the materials to make them are still the same, including mohair.

Fake fur

However, many kinds of fabrics can be used. Wool, fake fur, and many kinds of cloth are some options. All of the materials are soft. The fabric for teddy bears is chosen to last a long time.

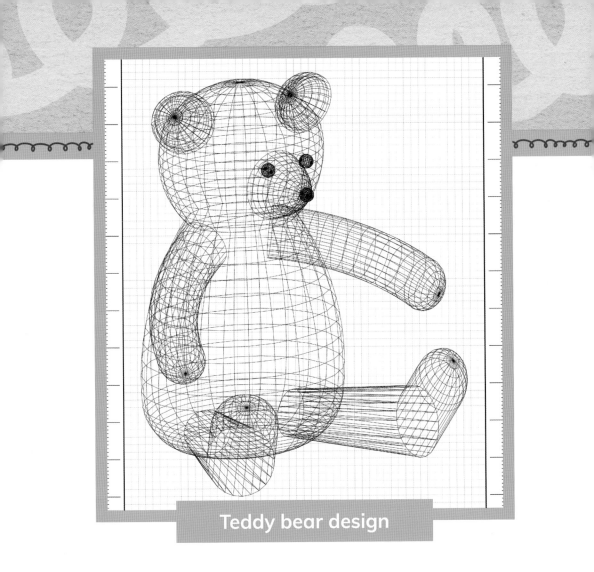

**Teddy bear design**

What is the first step in making a teddy bear? The design. A designer brainstorms what the bear should look like. They sketch it out. A designer makes lots of sketches before the final one.

A **pattern** is made from the final sketch. From there, a **prototype** is created. What's next? Making the actual teddy bear!

A pattern being drawn on fabric at the Steiff factory

Stuffed bears are made in factories. People and machines are part of the process. It starts with the bear's body parts.

Factories have huge rolls of fabric. They come in lots of different colors. Each part is cut out separately. Many layers of fabric can be cut all at once. This makes the process faster.

Some of the cutting tools are like cookie cutters. A worker uses a special machine to cut out the faces, bodies, arms, and legs. The faces have two small holes for the eyes.

So what happens to all of the cut-out pieces? They move to the sewing step. **Seamstresses** sew all the different parts. It takes a lot of training and skill.

Cut-out teddy bear pieces ready to be sewn together

Workers sew at the Steiff
toy factory in Germany.

The parts are often sewn inside out. Yes, inside out! It seems odd, but there's a reason. When the parts are flipped and sewn together, the stitches are hidden.

Now we need some stuffing! It is made of soft fiber. Polyester fiber is used to stuff most teddies. It is soft and gentle. It is easy to wash and dry.

Polyester fiber

A machine blows the fluffy material into the bear. A worker steps on a pedal. This controls how much material goes into the bear. The person can also control how fast the machine works.

Teddy bear part being stuffed

Now we have a stuffed bear, but it's not done yet. Final details are now sewn on it. Big bows. Silly hats. Other **accessories**. These are the fun details that make each bear special. Then teddy bears are tested. The parts need to be safe and secure.

At last, a cuddly teddy bear is born. But how do the plush toys reach stores? By being packaged in boxes and **distributed**!

# How Teddy Bears Get to Stores

Teddy bears are sold **wholesale**. This means that stores and businesses can buy many at once. They then sell the bears to their own customers. Teddy bears are made in all shapes and sizes. They get delivered in different sized boxes.

Some businesses let customers make their own teddy bear. People can choose the parts. They decide what fabric to use. They design what their bear will look like.

Teddy bears are a part of our everyday lives. One teddy bear flew on a space shuttle in 1995. Every year there is a National Teddy Bear Day on September 9. People all over the world collect them. The largest collection has more than 20,000!

The teddy bear is still one of the world's most popular toys. It will always have people's hearts. They're one of many everyday things used in our everyday lives.

# TEDDY BEAR BREATHING

Teddy bear breathing is a mindful way to help you feel calm. You can even do this before bed to relax.

1. Grab your teddy bear.

2. Get into a comfy position by lying down on the floor or your bed.

3. Shake out your feet and hands.

4. Place the teddy bear onto your tummy.

5. Now take a big breath in. Watch your bear move up.

6. Then take a big breath out. Watch your bear move down.

7. Keep taking deep breaths and watching your breathing buddy go up and down as you inhale and exhale.

8. Keep doing this until you feel calm and relaxed.

# GLOSSARY

**accessory** (Ak-SES-uh-ree)—a decorative item

**distribute** (dis-truh-BYOO)—the way something is delivered

**mohair** (MOH-hair)—fabric or yarn made from goat hair

**pattern** (PAT-ern)—a sample or model that you can copy from

**prototype** (PROH-tuh-type)—the first version of an invention that tests an idea to see if it will work

**seamstress** (SEEM-stris)—someone who sews

**wholesale** (HOHL-sayl)—the sale of goods in a large number

# READ MORE

Higgins, Nadia. *Toys Then and Now.* Minneapolis: Pogo, 2019.

Johnson, Robin. *Toys and Games in Different Places.* New York: Crabtree, 2018.

Sage, James. *Teddy: The Remarkable Tale of a President, a Cartoonist, a Toymaker and a Bear.* Toronto: Kids Can Press, 2019.

# INTERNET SITES

*The History of the Teddy Bear*
socialstudiesforkids.com/articles/cultures/teddy_bear_history.htm

*Kiddle: Teddy Bear Facts for Kids*
kids.kiddle.co/Teddy_bear

*National Park Service: The Story of the Teddy Bear*
nps.gov/thrb/learn/historyculture/storyofteddybear.htm

# Index

# About the Author

Mae Respicio is a nonfiction writer and middle grade author whose novel, *The House That Lou Built*, won an Asian/Pacific American Libraries Association Honor Award and was an NPR Best Book. Mae lives with her family in California and some of her favorite everyday things include books, beaches, and ube ice cream.